Victoria's Travel TipZ Italian Style

by Victoria De Maio

Victoria's Travel TipZ Italian Style

Copyright © 2014–2017 Victoria De Maio. All rights reserved.

No part of this publication including the content, cover design, illustrations or graphics, may be reproduced, stored electronically, or transmitted in any way or form including physical, electronic, or otherwise without the expressed written consent of the author.

DISCLAIMER:

The content of this book is for informational purposes only. The author has made every effort to provide current and accurate information. Summaries, suggestions and tips are only recommendations by the author and no guarantee of results. The author will not be held liable for any unintentional errors or omissions that may be found.

Furthermore, the author accepts no responsibility for the quality or nature of the content found within any external websites linked throughout the text. The links are provided as a convenience to the reader and does not imply an official endorsement by the author unless specifically stated.

For permission requests, please contact the author:
Victoria@PostcardZfromVictoria.com

SECOND EDITION: November 2017

PRINTED IN THE UNITED STATES

Dedication

"Open my heart and you will see Graved inside of it, Italy."
- Robert Browning

To my grandparents, who left their native Italy to come to America for a new and better life.
To my loving and adoring parents who I miss every single day...
I hope that somehow, some way, you know how *very* grateful I am to you.

From the bottom of my heart, this is dedicated to you...

Grazie di cuore.

Introduction

Un buon principio fa un buon fine.
A good beginning makes a good ending.

Believe Me, You'll Say "Grazie" ...

Who wants to learn the hard way? *No way!* And whether it's your first (and possibly once-in-a-lifetime) or your fifth trip to Italy, I want this to be *your absolute best trip to Italy!* I want YOU to enjoy *la dolce vita* ("the sweet life") not frustration, disappointment, and/or culture shock.

I promise that my insider **Travel TipZ Italian Style** will give you practical, no-nonsense advice, minimize surprises (at least the unpleasant ones), *and* enhance and enrich your experience. After all, I want YOU to enjoy, appreciate and love Italy as much as I do!

Short, sweet and to the point, this is *your* essential and perfect companion for *your next trip* to *Bella Italia*. So, don't forget to take me along!

Andiamo! Let's go!

Table of Contents

Let's Talk About…

1. Eating: Food Rules 13

Food Does Rule in Italy 13

Eating is Serious Business (i.e., Forget Fast Food & What You Think is Italian Cuisine) 14

Eating Etiquette..15

Let's Eat! Mangia! Mangia! Mangia!................................16

Decisions, Decisions… 17

L'Ora di Mangiare (Meal Time) 18

Caffè Culture Basics or Caffè-tiquette............................20

Service, Tipping & Those Confusing Charges on Your Check 21

Markets, Specialty Shops & Such..................................23

2. Sleeping & Creature Comforts 25

Lodgings 26

Checking In 27

Check It Out 28

About the Toilette or Bagno 28

3. Spending & Shopping 31
Currency vs. Credit 32
Made in Italy 34

4. Connecting & Communicating 37
Technically Speaking 37
Lost in Translation? 39

5. Getting Around 41
In General… 42
On Foot 42
Going Public: Taxis, Trains, Metros & Buses 44
Behind the Wheel: The Unruly Rules of Driving 47

6. Seeing Italy's Sites 49
Plan Ahead! 49
Remember: I Told You So 50
Please… 52

7. Getting Converted 55
Numerically Speaking 55

8. Safety & Well-Being 57
Basics 57
Never-Evers 58
When in Doubt… 60

9. Some Things Never Change (and Never Should!) 61

This is the Old World 61

Only in Italy 62

It Might Be (a) Fine 63

10. Why You Came to Italy in the First Place 65

La Dolce Vita (The Sweet Life) is Where You Find It! 65

About Those "Touristy" Places 66

ASS-U-ME Nothing! 66

Summary 69

La Dolce Vita for YOU! 69

Bonus 71

More Expert TipZ 71

Appendix 81

A Few Helpful Words & Phrases Anyone Can & Should Learn 81

About Victoria De Maio 83

Acknowledgements 85

1. Eating: Food Rules

Food *Does* Rule in Italy

Si deve mangiare per vivere, non vivere per mangiare.
Eat to live, do not live to eat.

There's a reason why this is the longest section, Italians are very serious about food! La vita bella is personified and inextricably interwoven in the Italians' deep rooted celebration of food, family and friends.

Dining is more than a quick stop to stuff your face and fill your belly. It's a social occasion; a relaxed and convivial time to come together around the table, a time to enjoy and share a bountiful meal and each others' company. It's leisurely, noisy, and filled with laughter, stories, and good humor. It's literally and figuratively a time to break bread together.

One of the principal reasons why people so love Italy is for its marvelous cuisine. Your enjoyment will be enhanced exponentially if you are familiar with its **Food Rules**...

1. Eating: Food Rules

Eating is Serious Business (i.e., Forget Fast Food & What You *Think* is Italian Cuisine)

A tavola non si invecchia.
At the table with good friends and family, you don't become old.

- The slow food movement started here so…*slow down!* No hurrying or rushing here (except on the road, of course!).
- Local, seasonal, and organic i.e., farm-to-table is a way of life in Italy.
- Think fresh! Fresh! Fresh!
- Think simple, nutritious, delicious.
- Think *artigiano/artigianale;* sourced and produced locally and always with pride.
- A top court recently ruled that serving frozen food at a restaurant without explicitly labelling it as such is a crime. Now, that *is* a serious food rule!
- You won't find "Italian" food as you know it (i.e., no spaghetti and meatballs, no *fettuccine Alfredo*, no *"Italian"* salad dressing).
- Food is prepared with simple excellent ingredients. Hold the condiments and spices until you taste it.
- Neither olive oil nor butter are typically served with your bread. That's right, no dipping and no spreading. (So, please don't ask.)
- Salad dressing is oil, vinegar, salt and pepper, *period!*
- It could be the pits…in the olives, that is. Be careful when you take a bite!
- Pasta and meat dishes are not mixed (I repeat, *no* spaghetti and meatballs together).
- If you order seafood-based dishes, please don't ask for *parmesan* cheese or *any* cheese to sprinkle for that matter.
- You may be looking into the eyes of your meal! It's the way you know the fish is fresh…*really fresh!*
- Food isn't mixed on the plate. Dishes are served separately and are meant to be eaten and appreciated separately.

- You won't get a large spoon to "twirl" your pasta and please don't cut it either.
- Bread is used during the meal to clean your plate, *fa la scarpetta*.
- Italians love sweets, *dolci*, but you'll find that they aren't as sugary sweet as they can be elsewhere (especially in the U.S.).
- *Gelato* is NOT the same as ice cream (it's better!).
- You can't take it with you (you can forget doggie bags) although *"Take Away"* is popping up but not without controversy (e.g., Venice has banned *"Take Away"* in its historical center).

Eating Etiquette

Tutte le cose avvengono per chi sa aspettare.
All things come to those who wait.

- Eating is an *unhurried ritual*. If I am repeating myself, it's for a good reason!
- Italians are also very serious about table manners; what I would consider far more formal than we are accustomed to.
- You'll notice that Italians use cutlery to eat almost *everything*. It's really a marvel how they manage! (Even the children are quite handy with eating utensils.)
- Fresh fruit? Peel, cut and eat.
- Dining hours are *VERY* different here.
- Lunch (*pranzo*) is typically enjoyed in the early afternoon.
- Dinner (*cena*) is MUCH later. 5:00–6:00 p.m.? Sorry, restaurants aren't even open! No *Early Bird Specials* here! 7:00 p.m. is still early. If you show up hungry, you'll be staring at locked doors and empty tables. Dinner time begins around 8:00–8:30 p.m, *at the earliest*.

1. Eating: Food Rules

Let's Eat! Mangia! Mangia! Mangia!

Chi mangia bene vive bene.
He who eats well, lives well.

- Don't judge a restaurant by the outside. Often the most unassuming places are the best. Lack of "curb appeal" doesn't mean lack of fabulous and authentic cuisine.
- Some restaurants are closed on Mondays, some on Wednesdays. Check ahead to avoid disappointment.
- Recommendations for the best food? Ask a local for their favorites. (Also, there are outstanding apps by locals/ex-pats with excellent recommendations.)
- Seek out places where it looks like only locals go. (In other words, run when you see a large group of tourists crowding into a restaurant!)
- The closer you are to major tourist/popular sights the pricier it will be. Sometimes it's worth it for the experience. Just be aware that you are paying for the location and the view and enjoy it anyway!
- Most establishments have their menu *(menu or lista)* displayed outside.
- Don't be surprised when the menus are only in Italian (or if it's only on a blackboard).
- Beware of tourist *(turistico)* menus with photos of the food.
- Your dining choices will vary in prices and formality. You will choose from the menu which is usually *à la carte* and will include specials of the day *(piatti di giorni)*. Occasionally you will find *prix fixe* offerings.
- Go for local specialties and/or specialties of the day *(piatti di giorni)*. If specials of the day aren't listed, be sure to ask.
- You *won't* find the same food/dishes/specialties or wine varietals in every city or region. Again, ask for recommendations and go with local.
- *Believe it or not* you can find good food at unexpected places, e.g., airports, train stations and *Autogrills* (along the *autostradas*).

Decisions, Decisions…

Quando a Roma vai, fai come vedrai.
When in Rome, do as the Romans.

While the distinctions can be a bit blurred you can choose between the following types of dining establishments:

- A *bar* is an informal *cafe* with a counter. *Bar* isn't like a bar as we typically think of it where you go for happy hour and drinks. It's where you can get an *espresso* and/or quick snack (mostly breakfast and sandwiches).
- A *tavola calda* (literally, "hot table") is a *bar* that also serves hot food.
- *Bars/cafes* will often have signs with two prices displayed: one for *banco* (stand) and one for *tavola* (sit). It costs more to sit, less to stand. (If you pay to stand, you cannot then go and sit down.)
- *Osteria* or *pizzeria* is informal dining with seating in a relaxed atmosphere. They are typically family-owned, family-style and inexpensive.
- *Trattoria* is often family-owned and run, medium priced and affordable with a casual atmosphere.
- *Ristorante* is fancier with more formal dining and service, and a more gourmet menu. Generally, it is also the priciest and often reserved for special occasions.
- The *gelateria* is the Italian ice cream shop (although *gelato* is very different than ice cream and, in my humble opinion, far superior). You will find a mouth-watering display and array of flavors (*gusti*) as well as other sweet tooth delights, so maybe you should eat dessert first?
- Typically at a *bar, tavola calda, pizzeria* and *gelateria;* first you decide what you want and pay the cashier (*cassa*). Then take your receipt (*scontrino*) to the counter to order, and to pick up your food and drink.

1. Eating: Food Rules

- Learn to stand like the locals do (although sometimes you just want to take a break or your feet are killing you and it's worth paying a little more to rest!).
- Italians don't really snack but tourists do so you may find occasional *"Take Away"* fast food places (a trend, by the way, that is nothing short of controversial). Once in a while there's a McDonald's in large cities. I can only hope that you choose to avoid them.

Everybody's Favorite - Pizza!

- You'll see numerous *pizzerias* with mouthwatering displays of fresh pizza.
- Pizza is served by the slice (*al taglio*) in *pizzerias* and *tavole calde*.
- Since it's served informally, feel free to eat informally. Enjoy, be messy!
- You will also find pizza offered on the menu of many restaurants.
- You may be ordering a full-sized or "individual" pizza. (Warning: Their idea of an "individual" serving can be quite generous!)
- It's fine to drink beer or soft drinks with pizza.

L'Ora di Mangiare (Meal Time)

Non è sano mangiare da solo.
It's not healthy to eat alone.

- *Cocktails (aperitivi)* such as *Campari, Prosecco, Aperol* or a *Negroni* are enjoyed before dinner and are not served without a little something to accompany them. It might be chips or nuts but it'll more likely be a complementary cheese/meat nibble.
- *Breakfast (colazione):* Typically Italians have a *cappuccino* and a sweet pastry (e.g., *un cornetto,* an Italian version of a *croissant*) for breakfast. No bacon and eggs, no waffles, no pancakes.
- You will get more than a *cappuccino* and *dolci* at your lodging but that's an accommodation for tourists, not a custom. The selection

may include pastries, granola/cereals, fresh fruit, cut meats and cheese, toast/rolls, juice and, perhaps, eggs on request.

Lunch (pranzo) and dinner (cena) are typically three course meals:

- Appetizers (*antipasti*) are *hors d'oeuvres* such as *bruschetta* and other local specialties.
- First plate (*primi*) is usually *pasta* or soup (*zuppa*).
- Second plate (*secondi*) is the main course which is generally meat or fish with an optional vegetable side dish *(contorno)*.
- Hopefully you have paced yourself so that you can enjoy some dessert? Dessert may be something sweet (*dolci*), or perhaps some fresh fruit, an *espresso* or an after dinner liqueur. (*Remember:* NO *cappuccino* after meals!)
- Only water or wine is enjoyed with dinner. (*Remember:* Beer and soft drinks are enjoyed with pizza.)
- Not sure which wine to order? Ask for a recommendation.
- Wine is offered by the glass and bottle as well as some other convenient options e.g., *un quarto carafe* (one-quarter bottle) and *un mezzo carafe* (one-half bottle), which is usually the house wine.
- Wine is typically high quality and inexpensive. The *vino di tavolo* (house wine) is typically quite good.

Yes, you can drink the water but...

- Water is not served with meals.
- If you want water, you will buy it by the bottle.
- Water choicies: *Naturale* (still or no gas) or *frizzante* (sparkling or with gas).
- No ice is served with the water (or in drinks).
- It's safe to refill water bottles at public fountains.

1. Eating: Food Rules

Caffè Culture Basics or Caffè-tiquette

Non si vive di solo pane.
One does not live by bread alone.

- Coffee is serious business (unless you're a tea drinker, of course!).
- A *cafe/bar* is where you GO, a *caffè* is what you DRINK!
- Sensational coffee menus/specialties can be confusing to the uninitiated. (In other words, forget *Starbucks* and those "half-caf, half-decaf *blahblahblahs*".)
- If you order a *caffè*, you will get an *espresso* (small, strong and black).
- If you order a *latte,* you will get milk. If you want a *latte* as you know it in the U.S., order a *caffè macchiato* (*espresso* with a little milk) or *caffè latte* (coffee with milk).
- A *cappuccino* is a frothy milky coffee sprinkled with cocoa enjoyed *only in the morning*.
- For the faint of heart and uninitiated, maybe start with a *caffè lungo* (an *espresso* made with about twice as much water) or an *Americano* (basically an *espresso* with more hot water added to it).
- Want decaf? Why bother? It's usually instant *Nescafé* (sorry, but it's terrible!).
- Need a real pick-me-up? Order a *caffè corretto* which has a shot of liqueur (typically *grappa*) in it.
- It's a BIG foodie *faux pas* to order a *cappuccino* after lunch time (some say after 10 a.m.). It is believed that milk after lunch disturbs your digestion.
- You won't find ridiculously priced *espresso* or coffee/specialty drinks.
- You will find delicious regional coffee specialties. Be sure to ask and give them a try. (Definitely try an *affogato!* It means "drowned" in Italian and your ice cream is drowned in a shot or two of *espresso*. *Oh my*, don't say I didn't warn you!)
- You won't see pots of coffee sitting on burners for hours. Coffee is *always* made fresh.

- Please don't say "to go". You won't see people walking around with styrofoam cups of coffee (although sadly in some places tradition is succumbing to tourism and styrofoam cups are options).

Service, Tipping & Those Confusing Charges on Your Check

Quando la pera è matura, casca da sé.
All things happen in their own good time.

Service & Tipping

- *Remember:* Here, *slow is good!* (Repeat after me…*slow is good!*)
- Meals are not hurried (and neither is the check, *il conto*). Is it slow or is it polite? Whatever, it probably is not what you are used to so…patience, *please*!
- You won't be rushed and you definitely won't get the bum's rush to empty/turn your table.
- As a rule you will not get the check until you ask for it.
- To signal that you would like your check; get the servers attention by making eye contact, nodding your head, raising your eyebrows and gesturing as if you're writing something on your hand or politely ask for *il conto*. And *please* smile!
- Note: You will probably have to ask more than once.
- *Please* don't shout "boy" or "hey you" or, when trying to pay, frantically wave your check and money in the air. (Yes, I have seen that done…*it wasn't you, was it?*)
- Again, *please* smile, relax and enjoy that glass of wine, *espresso* or dessert.
- Oh, and don't be surprised if you see dogs in public places, even in restaurants (the Department of Health here would go bonkers!).

Cover Charge vs. Service Charge Confusion

- Cover charge or *coperto* is a per person cover charge when you sit and eat. It's for the bread and silverware. It's usually a few euro per person and should be clearly itemized on the menu and on your check. (If you don't see it, ask).

- Service charge or s*ervizio* is exactly that, a service charge (perhaps 10-20%) for being served. It is automatically added to your tab. Again, this should be clearly itemized on the menu and a separate line item on your check.
- IF there is no *servizio* on your check, you can certainly leave a tip. 10% or a few coins is fine (much less than we're accustomed to in the U.S.). Use your discretion based on the service you received.
- That said, remember that being a waiter here is often a full-time profession, not just a student summer/part-time gig, so any gesture is appreciated.
- If your check is not itemized, ask them to provide you with one so that you can double check what you were and were not charged for.

✓ ***My Very Personal Note:*** There are so many conflicting tips about whether to and how much to tip. Unless the service/food is absolutely atrocious or ridiculously overpriced, I always leave a little *grazie* and encourage you to do the same.

Markets, Specialty Shops & Such

Chi non risica, non rosica.
Nothing ventured, nothing gained.

- Please look for fabulous street and indoor markets *(il mercato)* which always offer fresh and seasonal fruits and vegetables, meat, cheese, typical *(tipico)* foodstuffs, flowers, even sandwiches *(panini)*, housewares, linens, and clothing. (Most Italians still shop and buy fresh daily!)
- If you are shopping and decide to buy something at a market (e.g., fresh fruit), *look but do NOT touch (non tocare!)*. Ask the vendor/shop owner to assist you (or be prepared to be reprimanded and/or for very disapproving shakes of the head!).
- Be sure to explore neighborhoods and side streets, too. You will find fantastic specialty food shops in town centers and neighborhoods throughout Italy. Between the *salumeria* with its Italian style cured cold cuts, the *panetteria* with its fresh baked breads, and the *gastronomia* with an eye-popping array of cheeses, and take-out salads and main courses, you'll find yourself putting together your next impromptu snack or meal! And don't forget to visit the *pasticceria* (pastry shop), *enoteca* (wine shop) and *alimentari (grocery)* to round out your feast!

✓ ***My Very Personal Note***: Even if you're not hungry or looking for something to munch on, you absolutely must go in and enjoy looking! I dare you to walk out without buying a little something to snack on later or to bring home….

Buon Appetito!

2. Sleeping & Creature Comforts

Sogni d'oro.
Sweet dreams.

Nowadays there are many accommodation options but that also means being more discerning and doing a little research.

For some, a room is just a place to sleep and shower. For me, it's my space to relax, refresh and regroup. I want it to be reasonably priced, clean, friendly and in a good, convenient, safe location/neighborhood. Oh, and I want to get a good night's sleep (inasmuch as it's possible while traveling).

When you begin your search, it's good to know a few definitions and what you can expect when you arrive. You will also find that your local host often speaks/writes enough English for you to communicate via email with any questions and concerns.

2. Sleeping & Creature Comforts

Lodgings

Chi bene comincia è a metà dell'opera.
A good start is half the battle.

Albergo, pensione, bed & breakfast, agriturismo or masseria?

- *Albergo* is a full-service hotel with all of the amenities including a desk clerk/concierge, restaurant(s), etc.
- *Pensione* is a small guesthouse, often family-run, which offers breakfast and, sometimes, options for lunch and dinner (e.g., *half pensione* and *full pensione*).
- *Bed & Breakfast (B&B)* is a small lodging with (usually) less than 10 bedrooms. Often family-run as well, they offer overnight accommodations and breakfast.
- *Agriturismo* comes from agriculture + tourism. Since 1985 farmhouses/buildings have been restored and offer lodging (whole houses, apartments or rooms) and meals. They are working farms which customarily produce olive oil and/or wine, and the food is typically grown locally or on the farm.
- *Masseria* is the same as an *agriturismo* but is found in the southern regions.
- In the cities, space is at a premium so be prepared for buildings and rooms that may be smaller than you are used to.
- Italian law regulates central heating/air conditioning in hotels. There are specific limitations and dates mandated when they can be turned on and off in order to control and conserve national energy.
- Be prepared for stairs which are often steep and narrow (i.e., bring luggage you can lift, roll or drag).
- For those with physical limitations, be sure to confirm if there is a lift/elevator (*ascensore*). (Also confirm that it is operational.)
- Other stays: *Airbnb, VRBO* (Vacation Rentals by Owner), *Vacations Abroad, Homestay*, etc., offer options to rent and stay in villas, apartments, private homes, etc. (There are some helpful guidelines for selecting and booking on my blog.)

- What's in the "stars"? When you're searching for an accommodation on a search engine, there will be a "star" rating. Know that the rating isn't necessarily according to any particular standardized classifications nor is it necessarily consistent or reliable. The same goes for the comments. If you can get a strong personal referral or recommendation, all the better.

Checking In

- It's the law, Italian Public Security Code, and required that you show your passport when you check in and register in any lodging.
- Have and bring the names/contact information for all of your accommodations as well as your booking confirmations: (1) on your smartphone; (2) a hard copy you can refer to; (3) a copy you have emailed to yourself; and, (4) a copy you have emailed or given to someone back home.
- Always know the cancellation/refund policy especially if you book on-line or through a third party, i.e., read the fine print.
- When booking, be sure you understand if the room rates are being quoted in euros or your currency (e.g., USD, €). Remember if you book in euros, you will be charged at the currency exchange rate at the time of payment.
- Depending how many of those "stars" the lodging has, there is a per diem per person city tax on accommodations that is *not* included in your room rate. Typically from €1.50 - €3.50, this rate varies by region and by city. Be sure to check in advance since it will often have to be paid in cash.
- There is often a cash discount.
- Some smaller B&B's are cash only. For longer stays, ask if they will accept payment via PayPal in advance and offer to pay the 3% service fee (it's worth it so you don't have to carry a lot of cash).
- Breakfast (*colazione*) is often included but be sure to check. In pricier areas/properties there may be an additional charge.

Check It Out

- The lobby of any building is not the first floor, it is simply the lobby. Start counting on the next floor.
- *Ensuite* means there *is* a bathroom in your room (i.e., you're not sharing one down the hall).
- *Matrimoniale* (matrimonial) is a double or queen bed.
- Twin beds are often side by side, basically a divided queen.
- Rooms with twin beds are limited, especially in smaller properties.
- If you're traveling with someone you don't want to share the bed with or if sleeping side by side is just a little too cozy, you may want to opt for separate rooms.
- You won't find screens on the windows but they have fabulous shutters and double paned windows.
- You won't find boxes of tissues so bring your own or… well, improvise.
- Rooms almost always have hair dryers so I suggest you leave yours home. If you do bring personal appliances, be sure to get an adapter so you don't fry yours when you try to plug it in. (*See pg. 55, Getting Converted*)
- You won't find an ice machine so don't bother looking.

✓ ***My Very Personal Tip:*** If you want all of the amenities of a large hotel/hotel chain then you should book at a large hotel/hotel chain (and be prepared to pay large hotel prices).

About the *Toilette* or *Bagno*

Chi cerca trova.
Seek and you shall find.

In Private…

- The light switch for the *toilette/bagno* may be on the outside wall by the door.
- The bathroom/shower fixtures are terrific (once you figure them out).

- *Important:* Faucets will be labeled *C* and *F*. *C* is NOT COLD, it's *CALDO* = HOT and *F* = *FREDDO* or COLD. *Remember:* *C* = HOT, *F* = COLD
- Remember that many of these buildings are quite old and were built pre-indoor plumbing so the bathrooms could be "compact". Showers (and if there's a tub) will probably be small (so don't drop your soap!).
- That other fixture in the bathroom next to the toilet? It's a *bidet*, not a foot bath or ice bucket. If you don't know what a *bidet* is, look it up.
- Italians don't use wash cloths so don't look for one. If you just have to have one, bring your own.
- The heated towel racks are a terrific feature (not only to dry your towels but for drying those undies and socks that you hand wash).
- Recycling/water conservation is very common.
- Linens are not necessarily changed daily to conserve water/energy.
- If you want more linen changes, there will probably be a surcharge.
- Laundry facilities may be available or you can sometimes send it out for a fee. (My favorite facility is my bathroom sink.)
- Have you noticed all of that laundry hanging out on balconies and clothes lines in residential areas? It's because electricity is so expensive.

In Public...

- Out and about and hear nature calling? Find a nice little *bar/cafe*, order a *caffè*, buy a bottle of water or any little thing, then politely ask to use the *toilette/bagno*.
- Memorize this phrase: *Dov'è la toilette?* or *Dov'è il bagno?* (Where is the bathroom?) Most of the time, before you get the question out of your mouth, you will be pointed in the right direction.
- Once you find it be prepared for, well, almost anything (didn't I tell you to be adventurous?).
- *WC* is water closet, i.e., another name for *toilette*.
- Speaking of the *toilette (or WC)*, there may be only one so don't be surprised if it's co-ed. (Remember: *Forewarned is forearmed.*)

- Some places have public *toilettes* (will be clearly signed) and there is usually a small charge (usually 50 cents) which is definitely worth it.
- Sometimes there is an attendant with a small tray/dish to leave a tip. Please do. Trust me, they deserve it.
- Don't look for toilet seat covers or paper towels. They usually have hand dryers.
- Okay, I promised no-nonsense tips so I'm not sure how to put this delicately or if there's a way to but sometimes you won't even find a *toilet seat*. I know that this is not a problem for about one-half of the population; however, it can definitely pose a challenge to the other half, which happens to be my half! Therefore, my best recommendation is learn how to "squat" in a very ladylike way.
- There may not be a place to hang your purse or bags. Have a friend hold them or innovate (but *never* leave any belongings unattended).
- ALWAYS carry tissues/wipes. *Always* means *always*.
- Step, push, pull, turn, yank…you'll encounter a variety of ways to "flush". You may also see the 1-2 flush option. The smaller button is for small flushes and the larger is for…well, you can figure that out!
- Just don't pull the cord attached to a red button in the bathroom unless it's an emergency (near the toilet or in the shower) or you may not find yourself alone!

✓ ***My Very Personal Tip:*** When out and about, locate the closest *Toilette* ASAP. Please don't wait until you're in dire need, i.e., panic mode.

3. Spending & Shopping

It's important to be savvy about currency, ATMs and credit cards *before you leave*. Today it is extremely convenient but there are still guidelines you will want to be aware of. One of the most common mistakes I see travelers make is not bringing any or enough euros and/or not planning ahead for their immediate cash needs (minimum the first 2-3 days).

When it comes to shopping, Italy has spectacular style and shopping in Italy is fabulous! Although you may get a little sticker shock in some neighborhoods, window shopping is still fantastic and fun. Enjoy and be sure to budget for little (or big!) indulgences.

Oh, and another suggestion, when you budget for your trip, budget in euros.

3. Spending & Shopping

Currency vs. Credit

Ogni regola ha un'eccezione.
There is an exception to every rule.

Currency

- NO, you do not need nor should you bring *Travelers Cheques*! (Think *obsolete*. When is the last time you traveled?)
- YES, you need euros. Get some before you leave home (currency exchange, banks, etc.), *please*.
- You don't want to spend precious time looking for an ATM every day, do you?
- Please get smaller denominations (€20 or less). Small businesses don't appreciate large bills.
- And, *please* don't wait until you arrive at the airport; it's absolutely the worst exchange rate available.
- Don't expect to walk into a bank with a wad of hundred dollar bills and get euros.
- Always carry some coin and get used to what the euro looks like. It's easier with the paper money because the denominations are different colors, sizes, etc. Anything less than five euro is coin and although they are also slightly different in size, etc., it's harder to tell the difference.
- Cash is always preferred in Italy.
- Smaller shops and even accommodations not only prefer cash but will sometimes offer a better price/discount if you pay with cash.
- Italian shops, bars and even supermarkets have a purposely designed small plate or tray called a *piattino del resto* (literally, "change plate") next to the cash register where you put your money when paying cash. Your receipt and change will also be placed there.
- Spend all of your foreign coin before you come home (you can only change paper currency back to USD).

ATMs
- ATMs are golden and found just about everywhere. (Although whether they always in working order is another issue.)
- Many banks now have secured entrances to their ATMs.
- Know that even though you might have a certain daily ATM withdrawal limit at home, it will probably be less in Italy.
- There are usually bank fees and you can get double whammied, i.e., their bank *and* your bank may charge ATM transaction fees.
- Check with your bank *before* you leave to avoid expensive surprises on your bank statement.
- Transaction fees will typically be less if your bank partners with an Italian bank.

Credit
- Visa and MasterCard are pretty universally accepted here, less so American Express.
- That said, in many smaller towns and shops, they may only accept cash.
- Credit card companies will usually charge a *foreign transaction fee* when converting your purchase in euros to USD on your statement. It's worth the convenience.
- Check with your bank to see if they offer a credit card that does not charge foreign transaction fees.

✓ *My Very Personal Tip (and This One is a Pet Peeve)*:
When, due to poor planning, fellow travelers arrive without local currency and have to "borrow" from everyone until they can get to an ATM. (This can be compounded when time is spent looking for said ATM instead of enjoying a *gelato!*) So, I repeat, *please plan ahead!!*

3. Spending & Shopping

Made in Italy

Non si può piacere a tutti.
You can't please everybody.

- Shopping in Italy, even just window shopping, is paradise for the shopaholic and pretty wonderful for the rest of us.
- The four most important words to know when shopping: *Saldi* or *Sconti*=Sale; *Chiuso*=Closed; and, *Aperto*=Open.
- *Remember:* Leave room in your luggage for goodies you collect along the way. Even if you swear you won't succumb to temptation, I can guarantee that you will (and suggest that you do!).
- Many stores/shops still close in the afternoons (usually between 1:00 and 4:00 p.m.) and re-open in the late afternoon/early evening.
- Store hours may be posted but they can be more flexible in smaller towns (i.e., a family event may take priority over regular store hours).
- Forgot your toothbrush? Need cough medicine? The *Farmacia* is their drugstore but they're small and more like a pharmacy. Look for the large GREEN cross and take note of their hours.
- In small shops and in markets, the rule is "look but *don't touch*" (*Non Tocare!*). Please ask for help. In other words, no squeezing the tomatoes or manhandling every item (like you might do at home) or mussing up their carefully arranged displays.
- Don't expect to see the same local specialties/handicrafts/foodstuffs everywhere (e.g., ceramics in Deruta, linens in Positano, leather goods in Florence, blown glass in Venice, etc.).

In other words, if you want souvenirs, postcards, etc. *from* Florence, you'd best buy them *in* Florence.

- If you see something you absolutely love, go for it. You might not see it again, have time to go back or be able to find that shop again. (Been there, done that! Learned this one the hard way.)
- Look at the label to be sure it's a genuine "Made in Italy" (*Fatto in Italia*) item vs. the materials are from Italy but it was actually made elsewhere. Ask and then decide if you still want to purchase.
- There will be cheap imitations and knockoffs (especially from street vendors). Remember, if it's too good to be true, i.e., too inexpensive...
- Not sure? Ask. If you don't care, ok...BUT remember that it is illegal to sell OR buy counterfeit goods (e.g., Rolex, Prada, Chanel, Gucci, etc.). Fines can be up to 10,000 euros. Yikes, that's more than the real thing costs! And, even if you don't get caught in the act, you still need to get it through customs.
- Speaking of street vendors: Beware of persistent street vendors, once only in larger cities but now more visible in any town where there are tourists. Do not patronize or purchase - politely shake your head, say "no" and *do not* make eye contact or take out your wallet. (I'm pleased to say that during my recent visits to Florence and Rome, where they could be very annoying, local authorities were cracking down. *Grazie!*)
- Shoe and clothing sizes aren't the same. Warning: Their clothes are more "true to size". *Uhoh!*
- If you overdo it (yes, guilty as charged!), MailBoxes, Etc. are located throughout Italy. Not cheap but probably no more expensive than paying for overweight/extra baggage. I found them to be extremely efficient (my packages arrived home in three days!).
- What's VAT? It stands for *Value Added Tax* which is 20% in Italy. It's already included in your purchases (unlike the U.S., for example, where taxes are added on). If you spend at least €155 in one shop you can get a receipt and a form from the store clerk. You then take them, with the purchased goods, to the

Local Customs office at the airport *(before* you check in) and submit for a refund. (For advice and details, go to *www.global-blue.com* or *www.agenziadogane.gov.it)*

- Bringing it home: You love the wine, the cheese, that fabulous salami…you want to bring it home to share…Well, you cannot bring liquids (over 3 oz.) on board, remember? You can pack and check a few (read two) bottles of wine (suggest you wrap very well in bubble or dirty clothes). You can bring vacuum-sealed hard and semi-aged cheeses, chocolate, coffee, honey, canned goodies and vacuum sealed jars (check these through, too). It's another reason to bring lots of plastic bags. It's also another reason to take it all to a Mailboxes, Etc. (except wine or fluids) and let them ship it. In the case of wine and olive oil, have the vendor ship it to you. It can be pricey so you have to decide if it's worth it or not.

- Genoa airport is now allowing travelers to take as much as 500g of pesto in carry-on luggage, exempting them from the 100ml rule for liquids. Hopefully other airports will follow suit with local specialties…

- Always check with your airline for policies regarding number of bags and weight limits as well as current restrictions and limitations on what you can/cannot check/carry on.

- For a more specific and comprehensive list of items you can/cannot bring back into the U.S., go to *https://it.usembassy.gov/embassy-consulates/embassy/sections-offices/fas/bringingsending-food-alcohol-u-s/*

✓ ***My Very Personal Tip:*** Sometimes those *kitschy* souvenirs turn out to be fun little treasures when you get home and they make great inexpensive gifts. That said, I cannot emphasize enough how important it is to *buy locally made from local artisans!*

4. Connecting & Communicating

Despite all of the advances in communications and social media, and maybe because of them, we have to adapt to get plugged in. And despite the fact that English is pretty much considered the universal language, we have to keep in mind that *everyone does not speak and/or understand it*.

So, as the traveler and guest, being prepared on both fronts is highly recommended.

Technically Speaking

Volere è potere.
Where there's a will, there's a way.

- Get plugged in: They don't use the same voltage or outlets i.e. your electronics won't work if you don't "adapt". (*See pg. 55, Getting Converted*)
- Are you bringing *anything* that requires batteries? Be sure to bring them with you. (They're hard to find and expensive when you do.)
- Smartphones in Italy? *Sì!* The *telefonino* is everywhere!

4. Connecting & Communicating

- For international calling, every country has an international country code. Italy's is +39
- Cellular data plans vary and international calling can be pricey. Check with your carrier about a plan before you come home to a mega-bill!
- Getting an Italian phone or a SIM card: Sorry, you're on your own. I've never had any success but I know those who swear by it and you're welcome to try.
- To address the needs of citizens and tourists, Italy has recently (July 2017) launched a free nationwide WiFi app, WiFi Italia (http://wifi.italia.it/en/). The app, available on iTunes, *"will allow all users, both Italian and foreign"* to access a country-wide network. (Cross your fingers!)
- There are internet cafes.
- I suggest getting *WhatsApp* on your smartphone; it's a free app and you can message, make calls, and leave voice messages FREE to anyone in the world who also has the app. This is also the app most commonly used in Italy. (Note: It does require Wi-Fi.)
- Research using SKYPE, VIBER, or Magic Jack if you need to make/receive calls. (If you have an iPhone, FaceTime is also an option.)
- Have all of your contacts updated on your smartphone/devices. (I suggest also bringing hard copy "just in case".)
- Have contact info for the local embassy, as well as your airlines and local accommodations, etc. (*See pg. 57, Safety & Well-Being*)
- More good numbers to know: *General emergency=113; Polizia or Carabinieri=112; Ambulance=118*

Lost in Translation?

Si pigliano più mosche in una gocciola di miele che in un barile d'aceto.
You can catch more flies with honey than a barrel of vinegar.

- Everyone does *NOT* speak English, especially in smaller towns, shops, etc.
- *Remember:* Here, you're the one with the accent!
- You won't be understood just by speaking louder and slower.
- Also remember that Italy gets visitors and travelers from all over the world so a shopkeeper or waiter can hardly be expected to be fluent in multiple languages.
- Learn a few words, basic phrases and numbers, *per favore. (See pg. 81, Appendix: A Few Helpful Words & Phrases Anyone Can & Should Learn)*
- There are excellent translation apps but remember that you need Wi-Fi to use them.

Chi rispetta sarà rispettato.
Respect others and you will be respected.

- Listen, ask, *learn…*
- It's a courtesy to greet the shop/restaurant owner/staff with a friendly *buon giorno* (good day) or *buona sera* (good evening) when you enter. And it's a courtesy to say *grazie* (thank you) when you leave.
- Italians are very patient when you try to speak a little Italian. They even smile when you are slaughtering their lovely *lingua.* So, I encourage you to *just try*.
- Italians are warm and hospitable but private.
- Americans tend to be more outgoing, gregarious and forthcoming with strangers.
- Body language: watch theirs, watch your own. Literally!
- Animated and dramatic is normal.

4. Connecting & Communicating

- Loud is normal, everyone is NOT arguing.
- When in doubt, wait and watch a local.

Più delle parole pesano i fatti.
Actions speak louder than words.

✓ *My Very Personal Tip (which I have found to be failsafe):* A friendly smile and *buon giorno* or *buona sera* will break most communication barriers! Remember: *you are the guest!* Be a good one....

When asked what his secret is to making friends worldwide, *Anthony Bourdain* replied:

"It's pretty simple. Just show up and be grateful. Be a good guest. Be interested in the simple things. What people cook, what they eat, what makes them happy at the table - it's a very intimate conversation."

5. Getting Around

I have to admit that it's almost comforting (even amusing) to see other travelers standing on corners, sitting in *cafes* and wandering the streets, map in hand, with confused and even dazed expressions. You realize you're all in this together.

I'm not sure anything can prepare you for crossing a busy street in Rome or getting lost in Venice's labyrinth of alleys despite your Google map, handy dandy app or a map carefully highlighted with directions. I can say that knowing about what to expect and being as prepared as you can for it makes it more of an adventure than a frustrating, exhausting experience. And just think of the great stories you'll have to tell!

Remember when I told you to pack your patience and a sense of humor? Now's the time to unpack them! So, grab a *gelato* and let's go!

Chi va piano, va sano e va lontano.
He who goes softly, goes safely; he who goes safely, goes far, i.e., slowly but surely.

5. Getting Around

In General...

- Be prepared to feel *unprepared!*
- The unruly rules of the road; in other words, forget everything you learned in drivers ed.
- *Attenzione!=Attention!* It's a warning to pay attention which is a really good idea all of the time.
- Red can mean *maybe*, green can mean *maybe*…so, whether you're driving or walking, *always proceed with caution*.
- Get a *really* good map and directions. Don't just rely on apps in case you don't have Wi-Fi. (Some apps don't rely on Wi-Fi but, personally, I don't like relying solely on my smartphone.)
- Before you set out, have the name, address, and contact info for your accommodation either in your contact list (on your smartphone) *and/or* carry their business card. (This is so you can get back!)
- Look at the map and mark your route BEFORE you start out and have the name and address of your destination clearly indicated or written down.
- If you're traveling with someone or in a group, always have a plan B in case you get separated (e.g., a meeting time and place).
- Italy has excellent and affordable public transportation; trains, metros, buses, taxis, etc.
- Transportation passes are often included/available with city passes.

On Foot

Chi ha fretta vada piano.
Make haste slowly.

- Expect to walk a LOT!
- Wear good, comfortable shoes that you have already broken in but bring bandaids and cab fare *just in case*.
- No leather soles and no fancy heels. Yes, Italian women have mastered walking in high heels on every conceivable walking

surface and it's definitely a talent to be admired. For the rest of us, enjoy watching and attempt at your own risk.
- Pay attention and *watch your step!* You will find LOTS of uneven walking surfaces; streets, walkways, floors, sidewalks and so forth. Uneven pavement, cobblestones of varying sizes and large stone blocks which are often hundreds of years old can be tricky, if not downright harrowing, to navigate.
- Many streets are very narrow with even narrower/non-existent sidewalks.
- Be prepared for stairs and lots of them. They can be steep, uneven, worn and even a bit slick. One sprained ankle or pratfall could definitely spoil your vacation.
- Pedestrians beware: You do NOT always have the right of way even when it's a designated pedestrian crosswalk and the light is "green".
- Unless you feel like playing chicken with a speeding Fiat, follow someone else and let them cross first.
- Watch out for *anything* on wheels.
- The *"dieci minuti"* mantra! It seems that everything will arrive in 10 minutes or is 10 minutes away...well, not always...as a matter of fact, seldom... (So, don't take it literally when a local tells you "it's only a 10 minute walk" since that assumes you won't get lost.)
- Pedestrian-only zones and *piazzas* are friendlier and provide calmer conditions.

Chi la dura la vince.
He that endureth overcomes.

- Maps and directions can be confusing and can't possibly show every *via* and *calle* (especially in larger cities which often feel like mazes.)
- Have your destination clearly marked on a map and written down. (I know, I'm repeating myself so, *please*...)
- Street names can and do change at every corner and/or intersection. *Literally!*

5. Getting Around

- Take note of landmarks (such as a church, store window, or *cafe*) along your route, i.e., *pay attention!*
- If you get lost: Find a place to stop, collect your thoughts, and get your bearings (e.g., a *bar/cafe*, church or hotel lobby).
- Learn how to ask for simple directions to where you're going (e.g., *Dov'è il Vaticano? Sinistra* is left, *destra* is right and *diritto* is straight ahead). (*See pg. 81, Appendix: A Few Helpful Words & Phrases Anyone Can & Should Learn*)
- Italians will go out of their way to give you directions. They'll even walk outside, take you to the intersection, and explain as best they can with all of the appropriate gestures.
- Know that you'll probably still get a little (or maybe a lot) lost and try to make an adventure out of it. You may come across delightful places to enjoy a pleasant *caffè* or *gelato*, do a little shopping, meet friendly locals and have a story to tell when you get home.

✓ ***My Very Personal Tip:*** If all else fails, find a taxi station and spring for cab fare.

Going Public: Taxis, Trains, Metros & Buses

Tra il dire e il fare c'è di mezzo il mare.
Easier said than done.

Lo Sciopero! (Strike!) is a word you don't want to see! Italy is famous for last minute, usually short-lived, strikes. Sometimes they are even announced and publicized in advance for your convenience or frustration, whatever the case may be.

Taxis
- You *don't* flag down taxis here. This isn't New York City.
- Have your accommodation call for a taxi for you or, if you're out and about, find the location of the nearest authorized taxi station.
- Go ONLY to an authorized taxi stand and go to the first taxi in line.

- Before you get in the taxi, ask for the approximate fare to get to your destination (this is when it helps to speak a little Italian because most taxi drivers speak very little English).
- Just in case: Have everything written down and show them where you want to go so that there are no misunderstandings.
- When you get in, make sure the meter has been reset to the base fare (usually around €3).
- There are usually set fares to/from airports so be sure to ask and confirm.
- There are surcharges on Sundays, late nights, and usually for excess luggage.

Trains

- Train travel is extremely common and efficient in Italy. Italians may have a more relaxed sense of time but the trains DO run on time (most of the time).
- There are two great train systems: *Trenitalia* and *Italo*. Trenitalia (*www.trenitalia.com*) is run by the government and Italo (*www.italotreno.it/en*) is privately run (by the owners of *Ferrari*) but they operate out of the same stations and follow many of the same routes.
- You can book reservations on line: *www.italiarail.com*.
- Whenever possible look for the high speed *(alta velòcita)* trains (e.g., *Italo, Eurostar, Le Frecce*) which offer the fastest travel times and minimal stops. The Intercity trains are much slower but are often the only option for travel between smaller towns.
- Traveling second class is quite satisfactory in Italy.
- Train talk: Familiarize yourself with a few basic words. Train station is *stazione*, ticket is *biglietto*, train platform/track is *binario*.
- Repeat: You will not find elevators (*ascensore*) that work all of the time. Be prepared to walk up and down (steep) stairs (especially in train stations) with all of your bags and luggage in tow.
- Check and *double-check* the schedule since changes are made on a frequent basis.
- Every train station has a large arrival (*arrivo*)/departure (*partenza*) board displaying the current schedule (within 15-30

minutes of departure time). It will show the train numbers, destinations, times, and the platforms/tracks.
- Times are displayed using the 24-hour international clock. (*See pg. 55, Getting Converted*)
- The final destination and the stops are shown on the board. Be sure to check that you are getting on the correct train and coach.
- Validate your ticket (except for *Italo*) before you board and have it ready to show to the conductor or you could be fined. The time-stamp machine is located at the entrance to the train platforms. For *Italo* the conductor will validate your ticket on board.

Metros & Buses
- If you get a city pass, it will often include metros, buses, etc.
- Depending on your needs, e.g., how long you will be visiting, it's advised to research your options in advance.
- If you don't get or need a pass, tickets are inexpensive.
- Bus and metro tickets/passes can be purchased at the station or at *Tabacchi* (tobacco) shops (look for a sign with a large white "T" and blue or black background). Tickets are also available at newspaper/magazine kiosks. (Ask at your accommodation for the nearest and most convenient location.)
- Have your ticket or pass when you board and be sure to validate it at the time stamp machine (watch someone else do it).
- In Venice, you will use the *vaporetto* or public passenger boats. You can buy passes that are quite reasonable and convenient. You must validate your ticket before you board.

Caution: **Public transportation can be crowded and, hence, a pickpocket's paradise. Be super vigilant and aware of your surroundings and belongings. This is NOT the time to check your wallet, look at your smartphone or to let down your guard.**

Behind the Wheel: The Unruly Rules of Driving

Si salvi chi può.
Every man for himself.

- You're thinking of driving? *Really*? Well, I would say that you've either driven here before and know what you're getting into, have nerves of steel or are naive and a little *pazzo* (crazy)! (Maybe all of the above?)
- Unless you're experienced and enjoy driving in Europe it isn't really recommended (especially in large cities).
- Car rentals are expensive as is fuel which is sold by the liter here.

If you insist:
- It's advisable to get an International Driving Permit (your local AAA can help you).
- Check with your auto insurance at home to be sure if you're covered overseas and what coverage you will need in Italy.
- Most rental cars will have manual transmissions (stick shift). If you want/prefer an automatic be sure to request it.
- Learn the "rules" of the road and international signage.
- GPS has definitely helped to reduce the odds of getting totally lost but, I suggest that you cover your bets, i.e., have a map and learn how to ask for directions.
- Driving in cities? Organized chaos! The driving rules (what rules?) are "understood" and you probably won't understand them.
- Driving on the *autostrada*: Speed limits? Well, there are signs. It's pretty much pedal to the metal and don't even think about dawdling in the fast lane. Tailgating takes on a whole new definition here so keep your eyes on the road, not the rearview mirror.
- *Red* light and *green* light are merely *suggestions*. (And that's a direct quote from an Italian by the way!) I'm not sure what *yellow* means?

5. Getting Around

- Lanes? Hah! Right of way? Really? Turn signals? Please, what fun would that be?!
- Oh, by the way, don't panic when you see vehicles straddling the white line on *autostradas/* highways. If it makes you nervous, hang back if you're driving or look out the window and try to enjoy the scenery!
- In a roundabout way…there are LOTS of roundabouts (and confusing intersections) and merging traffic can be tricky. If there is a *"right of way"*, it basically goes to whoever hits the gas pedal the fastest! Hesitate and you wait…and you frustrate the driver behind you who is pretty quick to hit the horn. Best advice: take a deep breath, nudge in, then *go…*
- Parking rules? *Rules?* Parking can be very inventive. In larger cities, it's at a premium and pretty much wherever you can squeeze in and it's definitely a skill to be appreciated (although emulating is a different story, *si?*).
- In smaller villages you will typically have to park in designated areas outside the city walls.
- Be sure to always lock your car and stash/lock all of your belongings in the trunk. Rental cars are easy to identify and targets for petty thieves.
- And as far as traveling on two wheels? You won't find designated bike lanes here. Ride two wheels (pedal or motorized) at your own risk.
- Beware of *APE Cars;* those slow three-wheeled vehicles. (The driver may not have a license since one isn't required to drive one).
- After all is said and done though, Italians are excellent drivers and there are very few accidents. (There's no doubt in my mind why some of the most famous race car drivers have been Italians.)

In Bocca al Lupo
"Good Luck!"

6. Seeing Italy's Sites

After all, isn't this why you came to Italy in the first place? Besides for the food? With more UNESCO (World Heritage) Sites than any other country, Italy is a virtual treasure trove of art and *you'll want to see it all!* I don't want to burst your bubble but the reality is that *you simply cannot!*

Oh, I know you'll think that you can and will probably try…but you'll be disappointed. You'll be rushing, jamming, cramming…and missing the essence of what Italy is really all about: *Enjoying and appreciating what you do see.*

So, I have some helpful suggestions for you and you will see them repeated in the *Expert TipZ* (page 71)…

Plan Ahead!

L'uccello mattiniero cattura il verme.
The early bird catches the worm.

- My best advice: *Plan ahead*…I repeat…***plan ahead****!*

5. Getting Around

- Prioritize, pick and choose; *really enjoy what you do see*.
- Pace yourself: Do NOT over schedule!
- You've heard of culture shock? Well, you can also get culture overload.
- Many museums and major sights are closed on Mondays and for certain holidays but they may have extended hours on certain days, too. State museums, for example, are free the first Sunday of the month. Local museums in smaller towns can be iffy. Just to be sure, check with the museum or local tourism board.
- They actually observe holidays here. Again, check dates to avoid disappointment (e.g., April 25, May 1, and the day after Easter Sunday are local holidays).
- There will be lines and crowds at popular destinations/sights/museums *year round*, it's just worse in high season. (You can read more about the best time to plan your trip to Italy on my blog but think off season if you can!)
- Lines can be a bit unruly, too. Don't expect neat queues. *Queues?* Neat orderly lines? The concept doesn't exist here and if you do expect neat and organized, you'll be frustrated. Lines are a bit like how they drive so be prepared to nudge and squeeze your way through. Don't be shy, say *scusi*, smile, hold your ground and make your way through the crowd.
- Getting to museums and popular sights *early* or opting for a *late afternoon/early evening* visit is a good strategy, but the best plan of action is…

Remember: I Told You So

Meglio un uovo oggi che una gallina domani.
A bird in the hand is worth two in the bush.

- City/museum city passes in larger cities are a great value and can save you lots of time and $$.

- A city/museum pass allows you to enter any time you wish through a separate line, *the short line*. It's definitely worth it! Trust me: You'll be happy when you *"skip the line"* and waltz in!
- If you don't get a pass you can sometimes get reservations, passes or tickets in advance online. I suggest you try to do it before you arrive or enlist the help of your *concierge* or accommodation host.
- Having a private/small group tour with a qualified tour guide/company is the ultimate "worth it!".
- Go with reputable local companies/experts for guided tours that offer *skip the line* entry and include entrance fees. (You don't want to waste precious vacation time standing in long tedious lines, do you?)
- Tour guides here are extremely qualified. Not only are they typically art history majors/graduates but they have to be certified and licensed *and* take and pass quite rigorous exams.
- Local audio guides are excellent so get your nose out of the guidebook and take advantage of local resources. It's far more rewarding to look and listen than reading a book and trying to self-guide.
- Tours and audios are alway offered in multiple languages.
- Don't bring a backpack to a museum; you'll waste time in lines checking it in and picking it up.
- If you can, take advantage of and enjoy wonderful local cultural events, festivals, etc. Check event calendars in advance. (Remember this can also mean larger crowds which makes planning ahead even more critical.)
- Local boards of tourism are good resources and they all have websites.
- There will be restoration and renovation in progress. After all, if you were a few thousand years old you'd need some work done, too!
- A guide book is just that…a *GUIDE!* Not a bible!
- Budget for unforeseen splurges and little indulgences.
- Some places/events are worth the price of admission (e.g., an opera at *La Scala* in Milan, an *aperitivo* at the *Florian* in *Piazza*

San Marco in Venice; a glass of vino at *Rivoire* in *Piazza del Signoria* in Florence…) And I say, take that *gondola* ride in Venice and enjoy it! Pricey? Sure! Worth it? Absolutely!

- So what if it's a touristy *cliché?* Is that always a bad thing? I don't think so.

✓ ***My Very Personal Tip:*** This is not the time to penny pinch or be a grinch! This is once in a lifetime and what price for a priceless, i.e., a *once-in-a-lifetime* experience? Don't miss out, don't have regrets…this is how memories are made!

Please…

Chi cento ne fa, una ne aspetti.
What goes around comes around.

- Show a little R-E-S-P-E-C-T! *P-L-E-A-S-E!*
- Over the past years many cities/regions have been compelled to enact rules and restrictions to punish naughty tourists and to protect their precious cultural/historical treasures. (Read more in *It Might Be a Fine…*, p. 63.)
- Observe rules, guidelines and dress codes for entering churches and places of worship, e.g., cover up those shoulders and legs and please remove those baseball caps and hats.
- In churches, museums and major sights, when the sign says "NO PHOTOS", it really means *"NO PHOTOS"*. See that little camera with a red line drawn through it?? That means YOU! It can damage the art, for *crying-out-loud!*
- Likewise, "SILENCE PLEASE" means *"SILENCE PLEASE"*. *Yes, you, no talking…*
- The lives of saints (I think there's at least one for every day of the year), the Bible and mythology are the subject matter of much of the art and architecture here. Knowing a little bit about them can be enriching regardless of your beliefs (another reason why I highly recommend guided tours).

- If you're bringing children, be prepared to explain graphic and explicit images, e.g., nudity and violent scenes in the artworks.

✓ ***My Very Personal Tip:*** I see it *all too often*...Please don't spend all of your time taking photos or with your nose in the guidebook. Look up, look around, pause, people watch, soak it in, enjoy it...*now*!

7. Getting Converted

Missing a flight or connection, arranging for a transfer, charging your smartphone, showing up at the wrong time of day, looking for batteries, booking a train, reading the date or an address…these are all scenarios that are part of your travel planning and experience, and they all require knowing a few numbers…

Numerically Speaking

L'aritmetica non è opinione!
Arithmetic is not an opinion.

Time, Date, Degrees
- Learn to read time according to the 24-hour international/military clock, i.e., *no a.m. or p.m.* The easiest way to convert is to just subtract 12 from any number from 12 to 24. For example 13 o'clock international time would be 13-12 or 1:00 p.m. (0 hour is midnight, 12 is noon.)
- The 24-hour international clock is used in airports, train stations, etc. so it's very important to know and understand when making travel arrangements.
- Dates are written differently; the DAY is first, then the MONTH, then the YEAR or DAY/MONTH/YEAR. Example: June 12, 2018, would be written: 12/6/18 (it is not December 6, 2018). Again, this is very important when making any reservations.

- Temperatures are in centigrade. The conversion formula to get fahrenheit is to multiply by 1.8 and add 32. So, 22 °C (degrees centigrade) would be 22 x 1.8 + 32 or 71.6 °F (degrees fahrenheit). Personally I just double the centigrade, add 32 and subtract a few degrees and I'm close enough.

Addresses
- Addresses are written with the street name first followed by the street number. For example: *Via del Lago, 47* is #47 on *Via del Lago*.

Money
- You will be using euros (€) so €10,00 is the same of €10.00. They use a comma instead of a decimal point to separate dollars and cents. Likewise, an item costing €125.00 would be written €125,00.

Sizes, Measuring
- Shoe and clothing sizes are different. (Easy enough to find shoe size equivalent which is usually on the shoe box and you'll figure out the clothing as soon as you try something on!)
- Learn a few basic metric system terms and conversions: *litre* =a little more than a quart; *kilo*=2.2 pounds; *500 grams* is approximately one pound; *un etto* (100 *grams*) is approximately 3.5 ounces; 28 *grams*=1 ounce; a *meter* is slightly more than a yard and a *kilometer (km)*=5/8 mile.

Devices
- Get plugged in. You will probably need adapter(s), converter(s), or transformer(s) to use/charge all of your devices.
- They don't have the same voltage or outlets. Voltage here is 220v/50 so to operate a 110V device you will need an adapter (2 or 3 round prong).
- If you are bringing several devices (iPad, smartphone, camera, personal appliances, etc.) I suggest that you research what each will require. For more about electricity in Italy: goItaly.about.com
- Be sure that your adapter(s), etc. fit your device(s) before you leave home.

8. Safety & Well-Being

Oh, the stories I hear! And the warnings! I'm not sure why people love to share the story about the sister-in-law whose purse got snatched by a speeding Vespa 10 years ago or the uncle whose wallet got stolen by a six year old on the metro…

Yes, *of course*, I hear and read the news and headlines…but I also know that these are incidents and that they happen everywhere. So, my personal philosophy, and my advice to you, is the same when I travel as when I'm home: *always practice personal safety.* Be careful and cautious and, above all, pay attention and *never* let your guard down.

I would say use common sense but I'm sorry to say (and I quote) *"there is nothing so uncommon as common sense".* That said…

Basics

Uomo avvisato, mezzo salvato.
Forewarned is forearmed.

- Yes, you need a valid passport or ID (no visas are needed to travel in Italy).
- Your passport needs to be valid for six (6) months *from the date that you depart Italy.* (Example: If you're departing on May 15, 2018, your passport needs to valid until November 15, 2018.)

- U.S. citizens may enter Italy for up to 90 days for tourist or business purposes without a visa.
- Do not take your passport with you while sightseeing. It's recommended that you lock it up in the room safe or keep it safely hidden away.
- Take a copy and another ID (e.g., driver's license) with you.
- Make duplicate copies of all ID's including your passport, credit cards, emergency contacts, etc. Keep one with you, stash one in your luggage, and give one to someone at home. (It's also a good idea to scan and send a copy to yourself via email.)
- Most accommodations have safes in the room; use them.
- Don't carry more cash than you'll need that day. Again, use your safe or a hiding place in your belongings to stash your cash and valuables.
- Do you need a money belt? Up to you. Again, my advice is to not carry all of your cash in one place.
- Don't flash a lot of cash.
- Leave expensive/flashy/designer jewelry at home. (I don't even bring flashy costume jewelry.)
- Exercise common sense; this is for those of you who have it!
- Travel insurance? Get it. Now more than ever, it is *highly* recommended. It's an investment in your investment. It's also called *peace of mind!*

Never-Evers

Chi pecora si fa, il lupo se la mangia.
Those who make themselves sheep will be eaten by the wolf.

- *Never* ever EVER leave *any* belongings (luggage, purse, bags) unattended/unguarded, not *anywhere* at *anytime*! Not even for a nanosecond!
- Be discreet about your travel plans and where you're staying when chatting with strangers (especially if you're traveling solo).

- Never set your smartphone or other devices down on a counter or table.
- Never pull out your wallet or passport on the street or while riding public transportation.
- Don't burden yourself with oversized, bulky luggage or bags that are unwieldy. You should be able to lift, carry, roll up and down stairs, *and* fit into stalls (in airports and train stations), *everything* you have with you.
- No fanny packs, PLEASE!
- I'm not a fan of backpacks of any size. Deft pickpockets have devised all manner of techniques to lighten your load. Personally, I find them obnoxious when people turn around and forget they are slinging 50 pounds around.

Ladies

- Carry a cross-body purse with easy access (for you) to interior/ pockets, etc.
- If you're bringing water, maps, etc., I suggest you use a separate lightweight tote. You may also need it for small purchases and even for a coin purse so you aren't constantly opening/closing your purse.
- Go lightweight.
- NEVER hang your purse or bags over the back of a chair or on the chair next to you. (I always have my arm or leg looped through the strap when sitting down.)
- Don't draw attention to yourself with provocative clothing.

Gents

- Don't put your wallet or valuables in your back pocket. Actually, don't put in your front pocket either. Wear something with an inside pocket.
- Don't constantly check for your wallet which can actually indicate exactly where it is to a petty thief.

When in Doubt…

Fidarsi è bene, non fidarsi è meglio.
To trust is good, not to trust is better.

Regarding those rumors, warnings, and stories that you may have read or heard re: pick pockets, gypsies, unethical taxi drivers, con artists, and *(fill in the blank)* :

- Again, yes, of course there are incidents but criminals and wrongdoers aren't lurking around every corner.
- Keep in mind that Italy is a relatively safe and crime free country.
- The bottom line is that it is up to YOU to take the necessary precautions and be sure that you aren't a target!!
- *Blend in!* Sure it's still easy to spot a "tourist" but the more you blend in the better.
- Be vigilant and aware of your surroundings at *all* times.
- Always walk and carry yourself with confidence and a sense of knowing where you're going and what you're doing. (Even if you are lost and confused, fake it until you get your bearings.)
- Don't fall for scams such as people (often well-dressed) approaching you on the street or in train stations/on the train, for example, and asking if they can help you with your luggage.
- Do not be distracted by children or elders.
- Watch yourself in crowds where you can be jostled and distracted.
- Don't stop for panhandlers, street vendors or anyone that you feel is suspicious. (I suggest avoiding eye contact.)
- Someone should always know where you are.
- Carry emergency contact numbers with you. (*See pg. 55, Getting Converted*).
- ✓ **My Very Personal Tip**: *Practice personal safety ALL of the time!* Make it a habit and you won't be caught with your guard down in unfamiliar surroundings.

9. Some Things *Never* Change (and *Never* Should!)

Cambiano i suonatori ma la musica è sempre quella.
The melody's changed but the song remains the same.

This *is* the Old World

- Keep in mind that, although it has a history going back thousands of years, Italy as a unified country is younger than America! Each region was a city-state with its own dialect, customs, culture, etc. Part of this is a history of regional differences and rivalries which are alive and well to this day.
- Italy has survived invasions, wars, empires, monarchies, dictators, pestilence, and has graced the world with more art and beauty than (in my humble and personal opinion) any other country in the world.
- Time-honored traditions and beliefs are still observed as are national holidays and local festivals.
- Remember that you are in a country where the Catholic religion is practiced by over 90% of the population.
- In August most of Italy (and much of Europe) shuts down and takes *un buon ferie* (vacation).

- Family is *very* important. Since Italians aren't nearly as mobile as we are, you'll often see multiple generations and extended families together in work and leisure.
- You're proud of where you are from? Respect their pride in their country and customs.

Only in Italy

Vivi e lascia vivere.
Live and let live.

- Italians are well-known for being friendly, warm and generous. They are extremely hospitable and helpful; they want you to enjoy their beautiful country.
- *Baci e abbracci! Hugs and kisses!* Italians are openly affectionate; you may be greeted with a hug and/or friendly kisses on the cheeks by members of both sexes. Offer your left cheek first but be ready to take cues to avoid a head bump or awkward moment. This, as well as walking arm in arm, is common between all ages and sexes.
- Enjoy the *passeggiata,* the little walk. When stores and shops re-open in the late afternoon/early evening, friends and couples enjoy a leisurely evening stroll and perhaps an *aperitivo* before heading home or dining out.
- *Aperitivo* time is a time to socialize with family, friends and/or co-workers while enjoying a cocktail and perhaps a light *antipasto*.
- *Aperitivo* and *passeggiata* are fabulous people-watching opportunities, which is a favorite pastime here (and one of mine, too).

- *La dolce far niente* is "the sweet doing nothing" or "the sweetness of doing nothing"; slow down… what's your hurry?
- *La bella figura* is literally "the beautiful figure". Italy and Italians are known for their sense of style and this is personified in *la bella figura,* always putting forth one's best appearance. You'll rarely see sloppy here. So, save your workout clothes, flip flops, beach togs and baseball caps for the gym or beach where they belong.
- *Life is a bit of an opera.* Drama, emotion, gesturing, even a little theater…life is to be lived and lived with *passion!*
- *La vita è bella!* Life is beautiful! There is a genuine deep-rooted appreciation for beauty in all aspects of life whether it's expressed in the cut of a suit, the elegant lines of a car, a stunning window display, enjoying a wonderful meal with family and friends, admiring a lovely woman or appreciating a classic work of art. Surrounded by beauty, life *is* beautiful.

It Might Be (a) Fine

Il riso fa buon sangue.
Laughter is the best medicine.

What is normal or legal where you're from may not be the case here and could actually result in some hefty fines, if you get caught…but why would you be so foolish as to chance it? There's no doubt that heavily touristed cities and sites are being pushed to their limits and authorities have no choice but to impose regulations to discourage/prohibit inappropriate and destructive behavior. Don't be that bad-mannered tourist that we read about! Be aware of and observe local ordinances and laws. After all, isn't that what you would expect from tourists visiting where you live?

Vietato (forbidden):
- Milan has banned selfie sticks, cans, food trucks, and glass bottles.
- It's an offense to sit on steps or courtyards in Florence, or eat and drink near churches and other public buildings. Recently

9. Some Things Never Change (and Never Should!)

Florence officials have started hosing down steps of churches to discourage tourists from using them to loiter, eat and trash.
- Venice has a new #EnjoyRespectVenezia campaign reminding tourists not to loiter on bridges, swim in canals, or wear bathing suits in public.
- It's illegal to feed the pigeons in Venice or Lucca.
- In Genoa, it is against the law to walk around with a bottle of wine or a can of beer in your hand.
- In Rome, it's illegal to throw trash in a public fountain in Rome (as it should be!). And don't risk hefty fines by eating or drinking on the Spanish Steps or at any major sites such as the Colosseum or Pantheon.
- Beggars and panhandlers: The effort against begging has been taken up by many towns which have made it illegal for anyone to give money to beggars. It is actually forbidden to beg with children or animals and Venice, for example, has banned beggars.
- It is illegal to sell OR buy counterfeit goods (e.g., Rolex, Chanel, Prada, Gucci, etc.). Fines can be up to €10,000. And even if you don't get caught in the act, you still need to get it through customs. (*See pg. 31, Spending & Shopping*).
- If you're tempted to jump into a public fountain, it's now illegal and, for example, in Rome there can be a hefty fine (up to €200).
- I always wondered why men check their…well, their "package" so often. Well, it was believed that men could ward off evil just by grabbing their, yes, their crotch! However, it's now a law that they are not allowed to do so in public. *Footnote:* If a man pinches a woman, however, it is not against the law!

Although many of these offenses may seem harmless or even amusing, there is no doubt that they *are* offensive! In order for all of us to continue to enjoy *Bella Italia*, it is up to each of us to demonstrate respectful and common sense behavior, *sì?*

Così fan tutti.
That is the way of the world.

10. Why You Came to Italy in the First Place

Il mondo è bello perché è vario.
The world is beautiful because it's varied.

La Dolce Vita (The Sweet Life) is Where You Find It!

Why did you come to Italy in the first place? What is it about Italy that captures the imagination and touches so many of us? And what is it that resonates and can steal our heart? Maybe it's a romantic notion or fanciful dream…maybe it's a wish to live what we think is *la dolce vita*?

Of course, *la dolce vita* is in the eye of the beholder, *si?* So, as we seek the promise of *the sweet life*, it's important that we acknowledge and accept the bittersweet as well…

9. Some Things Never Change (and Never Should!)

About Those "Touristy" Places

Ogni medaglia ha il suo rovescio.
Every cloud has a silver lining.

- Yes, popular places are touristy…*hello?* You're a tourist, aren't you? Tourism is why they are still preserved and operating, why they are being restored, have staffs and are accessible for you to enjoy.
- Italy is the one of most popular tourist destinations in the world with almost 50 million visitors annually and only 60 million inhabitants. So, yes, there could be crowds, litter and a bit of chaos…
- I hear about the graffiti and how "dirty" Rome is (for example). *Geez*, so is New York! Besides the fact that it's a few thousand years old, with less than 3 million people Rome gets over 4 million visitors a year. Do you even want to hear about Venice with over 25 million visitors a year and only about 1/4 million residents with just 55,000 living in the historical center?!
- Certainly one should see Rome, Florence, and Venice but there are so many other "less touristy" regions and cities to enjoy as well, *sì*?

ASS-U-ME Nothing!

Il silenzio è d'oro e la parola è d'argento.
Speech is silver, silence is golden.

- Read that very carefully…and I repeat…*ass-u-me nothing*!
- Things *are* done differently here. You're the visitor, remember? Be a kind and respectful guest.
- Leave your preconceptions and expectations at home.
- Regarding stereotypes: Forget Hollywood's fictionalized, romanticized versions of Italian life, i.e., *Under the Tuscan Sun* and *Eat Pray Love*. And, don't expect scenes from *The Godfather*, *Goodfellas* or *The Sopranos* either. Remember that there are

- stereotypes about you, too! Yeah, how does it feel to be pigeonholed? 'Nuff said…*Capish*??
- You came to experience Italy, not to judge or compare it to home, *si*? Your experience will be much richer and gratifying if you take a little time to learn about your destination (which you are doing by reading these **TipZ**).
- OK, I just have to say it. My biggest pet peeve (well, one of them) is when I see the attitude of insensitive entitlement or superiority. Embarrassing and *UGH-ly!*
- *Si*, I have a new pet peeve and this may now rank as #1: Tourists behaving as if they were at an amusement park - in behavior and dress. Need you be reminded that these are historical, culture rich places to admire and RESPECT - this is *NOT* Las Vegas or Disneyland! So, leave your beach wear for the beach and your sloppy attitude at home. *Grazie!*
- Remember: rude is rude in any language.
- Don't compare or criticize: *"Well, back home, we blahblahblah"* (oh geez, who cares?) or *"Why don't they blahblahblah here?"* No no NO! If you want everything to be *like it is at home*, my advice? Stay home. It's that simple.
- Yes, Italian politics has its fair share of scandal and corruption and the bureaucracy isn't known for efficiency and timeliness… but who are we to talk?
- Remember the advice about not discussing religion or politics? *Si*, it's still good advice! You may have your beliefs and opinions but this isn't the time or place to express them, is it?
- You did pack your patience and a sense of humor, didn't you?

After all is said and done; if you come with an open mind, an open heart and embrace the differences, the Italian ways, your experience is guaranteed to be *molto bene!*

Tutto è bene quelche finisce bene.
All's well that ends well.

Summary

La Dolce Vita for YOU!

I love Italy! It's that simple. I love it and I'm *in love* with it; its beauty, its gifts, its contradictions, its charm, its idiosyncrasies, its heart and soul…

And it's because I love Italy and *I want you to love it, too*, that I was inspired to write and share these **TipZ** *(over 450 of them!)*. Is it meant to be the definitive, end-all, be-all guide? Of course not! That would be impossible and presumptuous to even attempt (nor would I even try!). Italy is far too rich, diverse and complex to be encapsulated in a few thousand words.

Since I first published my book, I have attained my dual citizenship and continued to travel to Italy many times. My affection and passion for the *Bel Paese* has never waned or wavered. I have, however, noted a trend that concerns me…namely, is Italy becoming a victim of her own beauty? Increased tourism has spawned some troubling trends (e.g., littering and loitering, climbing on statues, damaging artwork with selfie sticks, jumping in canals and public fountains).

Summary

Now, more than ever, I feel that my **TipZ** are timely and critically important in order to preserve and continue to enjoy this beautiful country and all of its precious, priceless treasures.

It is my heartfelt hope and intention that, armed with my **Travel TipZ Italian Style**, you will feel a little more prepared and inspired not only to visit or revisit Italy but to experience, respect, and delight in her wonderful ways.

I want you to savor *la dolce vita*, the sweet life, and perhaps, you will come to love Italy as much as I do!

Buon Viaggio!
Victoria

Let's stay in touch!
I invite and welcome your feedback and comments.

Please send me a postcard!
Victoria@PostcardZfromVictoria.com

Bonus

More Expert TipZ

La pratica vale più della grammatica.
Experience is the best teacher.

I've invited other Italy experts to contribute their best travel tips for someone visiting Italy. They all love Italy as much as I do and they all want you to have YOUR best experience ever!
   Some are native Italian business owners who work and deal with tourists on a daily basis, some are ex-pats and Italophiles who write/blog about Italy and who either live and work or travel to Italy on a frequent basis. And of course, we all share a passion for *Bella Italia*!

If you could give ONE tip to someone visiting Italy, what would it be?

Yle Sambati, Puglia Trip Designer & Owner, YLTOUR PR, Lecce:

   My travel tip for someone traveling (to Puglia) is: slow down and fully immerse in the local culture, releasing any fears and opening you up completely so that the language, the locals, the cuisine, the lifestyle truly becomes an experience, not just a trip.

Only by traveling this way you will find yourself surrounded by incredible people and live the most amazing travel experience.

Wide open, yet intimate, Puglia is pure serenity. Get to know this magical corner of this still undiscovered region. Immerse in the local culture and explore its enchanting historic towns through whitewashed villages, cook, taste, meet wonderful friendly locals, cycle through olive groves, dance pizzica. Combine this with fantastic food, incredible wine and lots of memorable moments.

Items that are absolute musts on your packing list to Puglia: sunglasses, your most beautiful smile and an open heart - but that doesn't take up any space which is good!

Make your trip be the expression of the many fascinating places and magical atmosphere of this region. Puglia is truly outstanding. Inspired?

www.yltourpr.com

Margie Miklas, Italophile, Writer/Blogger:

If I could impart only one suggestion or tip for someone traveling to Italy, it would be to go with the mindset of embracing the culture and lifestyle. It may be different from what you are accustomed to, so go with an open mind and heart. Do not go with expectations that life in Italy will be like life in your home country.

Let yourself experience the slower pace of life in Italy, the simpler lifestyle, and then allow yourself to meet the people who live it every day. It will be a life-changing adventure, and one you will always remember.

www.margieinitaly.com

Michela Riccarelli, Tour Leader, Pistoia, Tuscany:

Don't miss the chance to get in touch with locals: visit small towns where people are more authentic. Have an espresso coffee as they do: standing and talking about football, politics or fashion. Just listening, even if you don't understand Italian, you will catch the gestures and enjoy the real Italian spirit!

www.passion4tuscany.com, www.passion4food4fashion.wordpress.com

Emanuela Raggio, Co-Founder, BeautifuLiguria, Genoa:

"As a local specialist I would like to give you some tips about Cinque Terre:

-first of all Cinque Terre are a territory that deserves more than one day if you want to see something more that their most touristic side, so please avoid tiring day excursions from Florence or even from Rome!

- forget you car. You don't need it there and you wouldn't know where to park it. To move around the villages you can use trains or public boats. If you have a car you can park it in La Spezia but remember to book in advance

- Cinque Terre are famous for hiking trails but you have to keep in mind some essential rules:

- if you aren't a super trained hiker, it won't be possible to hike between all the villages in one day and, in any case, it would take you more than 8 hours just for hiking, without even stopping in the villages

-be prepared to climb very steep and above all, to steep descents with hundreds of steps. Be sure your knees are fit enough and wear hiking boots, not just sneakers!

-don't hike in Cinque Terre in July and August since temperatures are usually very high and there's a few shadow on the trails

-respect and don't touch the vineyards! You could damage the heroic work of local wine growers."

www.BeautifuLiguria.com

Anna Merulla, Co-Founder, BeautifuLiguria, Genoa:

"If I could give a suggestion to travelers coming to visit Liguria, aka the 'Italian Riviera', it would be 'Don't just limit yourself traveling to the Cinque Terre villages!'.

I mean, they are five beautiful villages but, there's more that worth being visited! For example: experience Genoa's medieval old town (the largest in Europe) and enter it's ultra-centenarian food shops and boutiques, don't miss the majesty of Via Garibaldi Unesco World Heritage site or try a slice of real genoese focaccia with cappuccino! I'm sure you'll fall in love with this historical town that has maintained its authentic essence and soul...and your visit will be much better with a local tour guide!"

www.BeautifuLiguria.com

Susan Van Allen, Italophile, Author, Tour Leader:

FLIRT. There's a shrink in New York who prescribes a trip to Italy for women who need a boost to their self esteem. Italian men have mastered the art of flirting - it's one of the city's masterpieces. Enjoy the stares, winks, the suggestive smiles, without taking any of it seriously. It's all in the spirit of: You are women, we are men. We are alive! And what a fun game we play!

www.susanvanallen.com

Monica Cesarato, Italian Foodie, Home Cook & Food Tour Guide, Venice:

Take your time, don't try to cram in too many cities and places in a short period of time. You can not see everything, Italy has got so much to offer. But trust me: better to see less but to truly enjoy it, than to see loads and not even being able to remember where you have been. The reason why 46 million tourists come to Italy every year is because there is so much beauty to see. A whole whirlwind of culture, art, wine, food and museums - a lifetime will not be enough. So, slow down, enjoy and appreciate what you will be able to see. If you have to bring back a memory of it, make it a good one!

www.monicacesarato.com, www.cookinvenice.com

Rick Zullo, Italophile, Writer, Blogger:

My one tip for anyone visiting Italy is to throw away the checklist and plan for a slower, more authentic experience. It is very hard to do this, I know, as Italy offers so many incredible "sites" that it can be tempting to try to see it all in one, two-week vacation. This is a big mistake, and unfortunately the most common one. As a result, the exhausted traveler returns home with a hard drive full of photos, but feeling like they didn't actually see anything.

Instead, stay at an agriturismo in Umbria, or at a masseria in Puglia. Plan days that revolve around lunch, not museum hours. Sure, you'll want to get out and see things. But see the piazzas, the markets, the local shops. The museums and monuments are great, but don't let them dictate your itinerary. Pick just a few of your 'musts', but otherwise don't bother with a checklist. If you try to see too much, you risk not really seeing anything at all.

www.rickzullo.com

Maria Pasquale, Director-Marketing & Social Media, Rome:

In Rome, visit Trastevere but put away your map. This is one of the prettiest districts along the banks of the Tiber river and with its narrow cobblestoned streets, certainly one of the most characteristic. Get lost in the neighborhood and breathe in the old Rome.

Get off the beaten path and take a break from being a tourist with us. Join us for a food tour or cooking class. You'll get to meet some Romans, eat delicious food and visit places that locals cherish but tourists rarely stumble upon.

www.eatingitalyfoodtours.com, www.heartrome.com

Orna O'Reilly, Travel Writer & Blogger, Ostuni:

"Visiting the Supermarket (supermercato): On arrival at the supermarket you will need a Euro for your shopping trolley, so keep some handy. Your trolley is released upon insertion of the Euro into a slot. On returning your cart to the trolley-park, your Euro pops out of the slot once more.

If you want to avoid pointed glares from the local shoppers, please use the plastic gloves provided for use in the fruit and vegetable aisles. You will find them on the same stand as the plastic bags. Fresh fruit and veg are usually piled high. Wearing a plastic *glove when making your selection is the regulation here, as the super-hygienic Italians dislike to see anybody touching their fruit and veg with their bare hands. Who knows where they've been!*

When selecting your fruit and veg you will notice a little sign with a different number for each item – say 185 for yellow peppers and so on. This is the code for your fresh produce. Place your bagged item on the weighing scales and key this number onto the screen. A stick-on label with a bar-code for swiping at checkout will be issued and you affix this to the bag.

At certain busy supermarket counters you will need to take a ticket to join a queue for the deli counter and for meat and fish. Look for the dispenser, take your number and keep an eye on the screen overhead or wait for the assistant to call out your number.

On checkout, you will need to have either brought your own shopping bag or you can purchase one there and then. Depending on the size and strength of the bag, they can cost anything from a few cents to a Euro."

Traveling Italy, www.ornaoreilly.com

Daniele Moroni, B & B Owner, Rome:

Italy can offer you a lot..cities like Rome, Florence, Venezia, Torino, Bologna, Pompei, Sorrento, the Amalfi, Coast, the Tuscan countryside, the Alps, the Lakes… History..Food..Art..Wine..Sun…Love :-)

My best tip…Do not stop to see just the above mentioned cities and sites, go all around Italy from the north to the south and enjoy the differences between the different regions. In each small village you will see something particular that makes it different from all the others, even if there is just a kilometer distance in between, it changes everything, even the accent!!

Go to discover the typical osteria where you still see our grandmothers making homemade pasta, enjoy what is local and take it easy because we are are Italians!!

www.bbaviewofrome.it/en/, www.smartrooms-srl.it

Francesca, Annalisa & Federico, Managers, Palazzo Belfiore & Palazzo San Niccolò, Florence:

"The best way to start to know Florence, you have to begin at the gardens. Start with Boboli, Bardini, Delle Rose, and the cypress beyond San Miniato.

Then, if you have time, you can discover a lot of secrets gardens in Florence and, if it is possible to visit several weeks during year, visit Giardino dei Semplici in Piazza San Marco, one of the oldest natural science gardens in the world.

Don't forget to have a little trip around the countryside of Florence - only half an hour away are many charming towns. The wonderful hills of Chianti such as

Castellina in Chianti, Casentino with Stia (the heart of textiles in the countryside), and the Mugello region, visiting Vicchio, and the home of Giotto.

Enjoy breakfast at a local bar with pastry and cappuccino, typical Italian style, to start your Florentine day and enjoy talking to locals… Take time for a simple and fast lunch of a sandwich and glass of wine at a local trattoria. For dinner you have the chance to search for and discover a new or old trattoria every time!

Visit Palazzo Vecchio, a symbol of Florence with its 'camminamento' on the roof and amazing 360 degree view.

Outside the main historical center, a visit to the Dilladdarno, Oltrarno or Santo Spirito neighhorhood is one the four of Florence. The color is white! It is divided in three 'rioni' San Niccolò, Santo Spirito and San Frediano. There is little market every morning in Santo Spirito square, and a lot of shops: vegetable, meat, seafood, bakery… mesticherie and above all artisans. You may see a lot of tourists, of course, but here people still live with family or friends. It is a little village inside Florence.

Enjoy Florence and Tuscany!"

www.PalazzoBelfiore.it, www.PalazzoSanNiccolò.it

Susan Nelson, Travel Writer and Advisor:

My travel tip is so simple, but made a big difference for me. I travel very light…one pull bag with 30 lbs. and a small backpack. So, with only a couple changes of clothes, I tend to feel dowdy after a while. I bring or buy lightweight scarves to hang around my neck. I feel so much better about myself…I just gotta have a little "dazzle" somewhere. And there is no added weight/storage.

www.timelessitaly.wordpress.com

Kathryn Occhipinti, Author, Conversational Italian for Travelers

"Why it is so important to learn a little Italian… Learn a few simple words in Italian to really experience all the 'dolce vita' (sweet life) Italy has to offer. Language is really about connecting with other people, and there is no better way to start a relationship than with a simple 'per favore' for 'please' and 'grazie' for 'thank you'. These simple words will elicit a smile from your Italian host and can open up worlds unseen to the 'just passing through' traveler.

When visiting an Italian restaurant, try a polite 'Vorremmo…' for, 'We would like…' when you place your order. Your Italian waiter may be so impressed with your understanding of Italian culture that he may offer a special appetizer or dessert from the chef 'gratis' (on the house) for their 'amici nuovi' (new friends).

Italians are a very friendly people who are proud of their way of life. They love revealing their favorite places to those who take the time to learn how to ask. A simple, 'Sa dov'e`…' for, 'Do you know where the … is?' will lead to the requested directions, usually with typical Italian gestures and some English to help with the translation. At times, you may even gain a friendly guide, who will not only lead you to your destination, but also point out a favorite café or shop along the way.

And, of course, who would want to miss the words, 'Ti amo!' for 'I love you!' if they stay in Italy long enough to meet that special someone? So, you see, knowing a few simple words in Italian could even change your life!"

www.LearnTravelItalian.com

Lora A., Owner, Savoring Italy

Lora offers several tips:

Don't skimp on the gelato! Trust me when I tell you, there will not be anything to compare to the gelato you will eat while in Italy. Please don't worry about the calories. You will hopefully be walking a lot on your trip and deserve a gelato break. I say, enjoy at least one a day!

Bring a journal to write down your thoughts about the trip and where you are eating and staying. Take lots of photos with your camera and your phone. When you're home, you could organize a really great album or posts online for yourself and for your friends and family to see.

Chat with the locals. I find that many Italians enjoy a chance to practice their English and you can brush up on your Italian.

Enjoy every moment and don't sweat the small things!

www.savoringitaly.com

Marilyn Ricci, Dual Citizen, Blogger

"Ciao tutti! I now live in Liguria along the coast of the Mediterranean Sea. Nearly every day I walk along the promenade where I enjoy people watching. Loving couples and entire families gather by the sea to experience la dolce vita.

I would love to photograph all those beautiful people that I see, especially the gorgeous children. I often do take photos but first I ask permission.

Always ask before shooting. Quite often they will say yes. If they say no, please respect their decision.

I have seen many tourist steal photos. Do not do it, especially of children. If you want a true Italian experience, ask for a group photo with these lovely people. They are very proud of their 'bella figura' and enjoy showing off for the camera. If they feel comfortable with you, if they see that you respect them, you could create quite the portfolio.

Grazie Mille and Ciao for Now!"

www.TakeMeHomeItaly.com

Shannon Kenny, Editor, Family Travel Resource Expert

When traveling to Italy with kids, a simpler approach to your itinerary will ultimately provide a richer experience for your entire family. We suggest avoiding too many transitions by determining 1-3 convenient central locations from which you can explore the sites you have in mind to visit, rather than switching your lodging every 2 or 3 nights. Kids will have a greater appreciation for the places you visit if they are given the time to settle in and explore at their own pace. Young ones tend to enjoy the simpler things that may pass us by as parents while we are so focused on seeing the things we have in mind visiting while abroad, whereas leaving free time for serendipitous encounters and adventures often produces the most memorable times together, and, in many cases, new friends. Leaving some unscheduled time in your schedule also allows you to seek advice from local Italians on dining, events or festivals, and family activities during your stay that you may not have had access to in your advanced planning stage.

www.italiakids.com

Lucia Restani, Italian Style Expert and Personal Shopper, London:

"As an Italian and style expert the ONE item that I recommend that should never be forgotten during a trip to Italy would be a beautiful shawl. People/tourists don't always see the usefulness of this item but, to me, it is the one thing I always have in my bag.

But why is this the piece I strongly suggest? Not everybody is aware of the fact that in most 'posti sacri' as churches, convents, etc. (which Italy is rich of) women are not allowed to enter with bare arms and short bottoms. So a cover up is necessary if you want to be sure to enjoy a visit to any religious building.

However, I'd never suggest anything that wouldn't also have a charming purpose. A beautiful shawl has the power to add a touch of glamour and personality to any outfit. Even the simplest dress or separates can be dressed up with a shawl. Also, let's not forget the drop of temperatures in the evening, the breeze by the coast or just the air conditioning in a restaurant... again, you'll find it very useful. Why not be appropriate, stylish and feminine?

So, if you still do not have a stunning one in your drawer, you might want to invest in one that you love in either a neutral colour or multicolour depending on what would *fit best in your wardrobe. And, you can have fun shopping and choosing from different materials depending on the season.*

Happy shopping!"

www.luciarestani.com

Nada Vergili, Owner, Nada's Italy Tours:

Here are 5 of Nada's Commandments for Traveling to Italy: Just follow these simple commandments and thou shalt hath a wonderful vacation!

Thou shalt never pass on the opportunity to use the restroom. When in need, look for a "Bar", purchase something (anything - juice, coffee, a pack of gum) and ask for the "Bagno".

Thou shalt not exchange money from an "Exchange" booth as you will get ripped off. Instead, thou shalt exchange US$ before leaving the US, or use your ATM/credit card in Italy.

Thou shalt not wear flashy jewelry, cameras, designer luggage, and other bright, high-end fashion items that may attract people with shady intentions.

(In a restaurant) Thou shalt not ask for: grated Parmesan for your salad and/or pizza, extra sauce for your pasta, cappuccino after lunch or dinner. Thou shalt not ask for pasta as your side dish. Thou shalt not ask for a "bistecca fiorentina" (Florentine steak) as well-done.

Thou shalt learn to correctly pronounce and use "Buongiorno" (good morning), "Per favore" (please), "Scusi" (excuse me), and "Grazie" (thank you).

www.nadasitaly.com

Appendix

A Few Helpful Words & Phrases Anyone Can & *Should* Learn

Chi molto pratica, molto impara.
Practice makes perfect.

Yes *Sì* (sEE)
No *No* (noh)
Good day *Buon giorno* (boo-OHn jee-OHr-noh)
Good evening *Buona sera* (boo-OH-nah sAYrah)
Please *Per piacere* (pEHr pee-ah-chAY-reh)
    Per favore (pehr fah-vOH-reh)
Thank you *Grazie* (grAH-tsee-eh)
You're welcome *Prego* (prEh-goh)
I would like… *Vorrei* (vohr-rEH-ee)
That's all right, okay *Va bene* (vah bEH-neh)
Excuse me *Mi scusi* (mee skOO-see)
Good bye *Arrivederci* (ahr-ree-veh-dAYr-chee)
Let's go! *Andiamo!* (ahn-dee-AH-moh)
Do you speak English? *Parla Inglese?* (paHr-lah een-glAY-seh?)
I don't understand *Non capisco* (nohn kah-pEE-skoh)

How much? *Quanto?* (koo AHn-toh)
How? *Come?* (kOH-meh)
When? *Quando?* (koo-AHn-doh)
Where is? *Dov'e?* (dOH-veh)
Why? *Perche?* (pehr-kAY)
I (don't) know. *(Non) lo so.* (nohn) loh sOH)
Entrance *Ingresso* (een-grEHs-soh)
Exit *Uscita* (oo-shEE-tah)

Emergency:
Help! *Aiuto!* (eye-YOO-toh)

Directions:
Left *sinistra* (ah see-nee-stray)
Right *destra* (ah dEH-strah)
Straight *diritto* (dee-rEEt-toh)

Numbers:
1 *uno* (OO-noh)
6 *sei* (sEH-ee)
2 *due* (dOO-eh)
7 *sette* (sEHt-teh)
3 *tre* (trEH)
8 *otto* (OHt-toh)
4 *quattro* (koo-AHt-troh)
9 *nove* (nOH-veh)
5 *cinque* (chEEn-koo-eh)
10 *dieci* (dee-EH-chee)

About Victoria De Maio

Travel Advisor, Writer, Blogger, Tour Leader

Cercare, gustare, amare la dolce vita - con passione!
Seeking, savoring, loving the sweet life - with passion!

La dolce vita for me sums up Victoria's passion and love for all things Italian. An American (with deep Italian roots and dual citizenship) living in California, her heart is *always* in Italy.

Victoria loves sharing practical no-nonsense travel tips and insights as well as her own experiences from a personal and light-hearted point-of-view on her travel blog, **PostcardZ from Victoria**. Needless to say, her favorite subject is Italy!

She is a regular contributing writer for *Italian Talks* and *L'Italo-Americano*, and guest writer for other travel blogs. She writes expert hotel reviews for *The Telegraph London* and *Forbes Travel Guide* and can be found on *Facebook, Twitter, LinkedIn, YouTube, Pinterest, Instagram* and, of course, on *Amazon*.

A proud member of the *Professional Travel Bloggers Association (PTBA)* and *The International Travel Writers Alliance (ITWA)*, Victoria is available for talks and book signings.

She would love to help *you* plan your next dream trip to Italy. *Better yet*, join her in Italy for a *fabulous, authentic, affordable, unique boutique* travel experience!

For more information, please contact Victoria:

Victoria@PostcardZfromVictoria.com

Please visit my blog, follow me and subscribe to my e-newsletter for updates:
www.PostcardZfromVictoria.com

Find Victoria on:
http://www.amazon.com/Victoria-De-Maio/e/B00PE9NYJG
http://www.italoamericano.org/author/Victoria+De+Maio
www.italiantalks.com/en/victoria
https://facebook.com/victoria.ladolcevita4me
https://www.linkedin.com/in/victoriademaiotravelpizazz
https://twitter.com/LaDolceVita4Me
http://www.YouTube.com/user/VictoriaTravelPiZazz
http://instagram.com/ladolcevitaforme
http://www.pinterest.com/victoriademaio

Acknowledgements

My heartfelt gratitude and *grazie* to all those who have and continue to provide moral support and encouragement for this and all of my endeavors. Your love and friendship are priceless treasures.

Grazie of gratitude to those who contributed their invaluable expertise and feedback.

To my *Lulu LaMew*, now in heaven, you will always be my beloved *la dolce far niente* expert and *Editor-in-Chief*.

To my creative friend Jen, of JLeMay Studios (www.jlemay.com), who designs all of my wonderful illustrations & graphics.

To Charlie of Charfish Design (www.charfishdesign.com) for his patience, humor and tech expertise.

Photo Credit: Victoria De Maio

And, of course, to the people of Italy; without you, where would my heart's home be??

Made in the USA
Las Vegas, NV
09 November 2020